If water breathes

If water breathes

Monika Hope Lee

RESOURCE *Publications* · Eugene, Oregon

IF WATER BREATHES

Copyright © 2019 Monika Hope Lee. All rights reserved. Except for brief quotations in critical publications or reviews, no part of this book may be reproduced in any manner without prior written permission from the publisher. Write: Permissions, Wipf and Stock Publishers, 199 W. 8th Ave., Suite 3, Eugene, OR 97401.

Resource Publications
An Imprint of Wipf and Stock Publishers
199 W. 8th Ave., Suite 3
Eugene, OR 97401

www.wipfandstock.com

PAPERBACK ISBN: 978-1-5326-7727-4
HARDCOVER ISBN: 978-1-5326-7728-1
EBOOK ISBN: 978-1-5326-7729-8

Manufactured in the U.S.A.

for Anna

Contents

Acknowledgements | xi

I: Light is Born
Follow | 2
Anna | 4
Brown god | 5
May | 6
September sun | 7
Autumn | 8
Twenty-third of November | 9
December | 10
Initiate | 11

II: Kalachakra
Barefoot | 14
Bicycles in Jaipur | 15
Ashram | 17
Dhyana | 18
Jams and chutneys | 19
Hanuman | 20
Ashoka | 21
Meera | 22
Kalachakra | 23

III: You

Our words are not at all the thoughts we dream | 26
At your departure | 27
Devolution | 28
Renaissance | 29
Wrens | 30
We ask too much of love | 31
Ramble | 32
Response | 34
Stellar collapse | 35

IV: Samsara

Waystation | 38
The walls of our house are blank | 39
Whoonu? | 40
Beginning | 42
Swim the waves | 44
Doctor Fish | 45
Palace El Badi, the Incomparable in Marrakech | 46
Mammal | 47
Southwestern Ontario Gothic | 48

V: The Garden Tomb

i cannot tell | 50
Body Double | 51
Artemis | 52
Ash Attic | 53
Penelope | 54
Boat-building | 55
Fledglings | 57
Tim Beck | 59
Ghost | 61

VI: Revelation

Originary | 64

Torn | 65

new born | 66

genesis | 67

Core | 68

Moksha | 69

Psalm | 71

Seven-Story Mountain | 73

Talking to the Unknowable | 74

I took the little book | 75

Bibliography | 77

Acknowledgements

Earlier versions of these poems have appeared in *vallum: contemporary poetry, The Windsor Review, Room, Feminist Studies, Open Minds Quarterly, Burning Tree Press, Scrivener Creative Review, Synaeresis: arts + poetry, Morel Magazine, Coldnoon: Travel Poetics, Afterthoughts,* and *Consciousness, Literature, and the Arts.* Thank you to these journals and their editors.

I gratefully acknowledge the support of the Ontario Arts Council whose Writers' Reserve grant enabled me to work on this collection of poems.

I extend heartfelt thanks to Brian Diemert, Marnie Parsons, Alvin A. Lee, Steven Heighton, John B. Lee, Nathan TeBokkel, Shelly Harder, Susan Downe, Julie Berry, John Tyndall, Patricia Black, James Doelman, Nancy Spring, Donna Rogers, John Mitchell, Dominick Grace, Deborah Pearson, Betty Juknys, Bella Bonnet, Anna Lee-Diemert, and Natasha Lee-Diemert.

Thank you to Poetry London and to *Afterthoughts* under Andreas Connel-Gripp for awarding prizes to former versions of "The walls of our house are blank" and "Anna" respectively. I offer deep thanks to Susan Merskey and Sheila Martindale at South Western Ontario Press for publishing my first collection of poems. I acknowledge with gratitude the support of Brescia University College, the Humber College School for Writers, and my faculty colleagues in the Brescia Writers' Group.

I
Light is Born

"Rocks, dens, and groves of foliage taught to melt
Into each other their obsequious hues,
Vanished and vanishing in subtle chase,
Too fine to be pursued."

—William Wordsworth, *The Prelude* 8.88-91.

Follow

A blackbird flies from tree to tree
not looking to see if they follow
black on blue.

Emergent, aligned
then   separating
they follow
           follow.
Raindrops

constellate on wings
altitude   direction
          shift
suddenly—

still they follow.
They dry in the sun as they move
insectivorous through swamps and brush
(follow   follow)

they glean and hover
hawk, peck, and probe
forage upright or hang

      midair.

I look behind to see if they are there
and still
     they follow

while I separate the wind
find the slipstream
and sometimes
     aloft, above, beyond
the sodden earth

while the chant of our song
moment by moment
sounds the echo we hear

we become the daybreak
and follow.

Anna

There's nothing like my love
asleep

swathed in cotton,
spotted with stars—

bare toes, clean and fresh as berries,
folding and curling in time with her breath,

a flannel quilt around her smallness,
her noise-white hum of present flesh.

There's nothing like my love
asleep;

her brow furls and unfurls,
a sail to ferry
mind-breezes, song-breath.

There's nothing like my love—

the mother-ocean on which she sails,
overturning, capsizing me.

Helpless in the offing,
I am washed here
to the shore of dream.

Brown god

Why are gods never painted brown?
Like the river, this brown god
whose reeds and trees of March are thinning hair.

And if a god, why doesn't he dis-
entangle his vegetation's doom
instead of clinging to last year's milkweed, cattails,
long dead but still with him?

Why does he hurry in spring
back to the source where he must
start anew?

He is old,
too old to care what you or I have lost.

He's wandered through more Aprils
than we'll ever know.

Some say he teaches humility;
his glassy mirror reflects
sun gems to eclipse the I.

To know a god
or leave a god,
when we are godless
sequestered in a feint.

May

We pull ourselves away
from the sipping, slipping
hungering throat
into lucent May.

We abandon cells
and solitary jails
for lawns with fluffs of gold,
air of silken filigree.

Renounce torpor
and choose pink –
eyes are windows
of magnolia and cherry blossom.

Let's forget we are poems,
while Gold Creek Pond calls me,
whispers my name in such tones.
If water breathes,
I believe it is in love.

September sun
for Dad

A golden sheen encompasses the wood
and blood red drops of maple spot the greens,
the leaning lights of autumn gleam with time—
kaleidoscopic splendor in the leaves.

A heron curls his neck into the pool
and eddies swirl beside his perfect form;
he sees us and he watches from his stance,
the water mirrors sunshine – light is born.

We sit upon a solid-seeming stump,
the warmth and sprays of blossom hold us there,
the spotted moment's wordless glory stays
and waters glisten in the clockless air.

A stream, a sky, the leaves, and we are one
resplendent glow beneath the midday sun.

Autumn

For we are the autumn
in feverish hues.

Leaves and golden corn
turn a green land yellow

to make a sun's brief days
more charmed and unabashed.

—and so I dreamed of
finishing the race

on a trolley of pine
and I was given a cup

filled with a honey-colored drink as
I saw the triumph of autumn

under boughs of blazing foliage
under swords of slanting light

a golden gleaming prize in
the art of dying time.

Twenty-third of November
for Mum

The sun makes a rare show
more muted than June's
its backdrop so pale.

There is no snow in Lobo;
dried perennial stalks spot flower beds;
the maples are naked and black on pallor.

No blizzard of one
no store of loss, no final good
bye.

Now, each day, ever after
coming, then taking
their leave, their
leave.

I know nothing
begin to know it intimately
in November sunlight
blinded.

Where did she—where has

I asked her once to haunt
me, but her only ghost
the insides of trees—
darkened corridors
held black on white, bare
waiting freckled,
over-exposed

blackened branches
perched on sky.

December

December speaks against stale fripperies,
bunched up foil and heaps of bags.
Her cool darkness strives
for discreet forms of death,
minds and threadbare memories.

December resists plastic trees and garlands,
their moratorium on the season's bruised insides.
Why not assume the proper burden
of cold and dwindling light?
Seasonal disorders are diurnal requirements,
the moon decrees, as she shines
on Demeter's willed and necessary break from love.

In defiance of electric snow globes
and felt reindeer, the unheeded month voices
its epicyclic truth
a patient prerogative of dearth.

Initiate

The blow of snow
the tinge of ice
the cat upon the hearth
who listens
once
twice

and I
I was quiet
as I reached
to touch the white
while the night
was growing colder
and the cat
twitched
like a flurry of light.

II

Kalachakra

"As a fish taken from his watery home and thrown on dry ground, our thought trembles all over."

—*Tibetan Dhammapada* 3.34.

Barefoot

One by one
we shuffle past the Bodhi tree
where Gautama awoke
and others sleep.

Shoeless and sockless, we walk past pilgrims,
rain and Indian mud sloshing our bare feet.

The threat of a parasite in the toe
exposes our beaded breath.

Too damp to burn
in the rain, we move.

White, blue, red and yellow
flags across Snake Lake.

Thousands of monk robes, mustard and maroon,
mandalas of saffron water and marigolds,
the prostrate on boards, on stone.

Suddenly you said,
"This is the Bodhi tree?"

Hidden behind your camera
you'd somehow missed
where we were
as we all tend to miss
the crucial thing,
each time we walk circles, barefoot
around the Bodhi tree.

Bicycles in Jaipur

*The brochure read: "a leisurely bike ride,
through countryside and small villages."*

We rode through midday traffic
in New and Old Jaipur—

city of jewels,
miniature paintings,
block printing, blue pottery,
bandhani, tourism,
cricket—
Rajasthan's capital,
pink city of terra
-cotta and white.

Concentrating every cell
on the task of staying alive,
we saw little of the mosques and minarets
still less of shops and artisanal crafts,
of painted stucco.

Jaipur became a bicycle
wheel,

nothing but obstacles
between us and *Man Sagar*
—scooters, rickshaws, tour buses,
cows, cars, camels;
people crisscrossed
like stitching on a rug.

We breathed bad air,
turquoise scarf tied over the mouth.

Focus on a turning wheel:
Jaipur was that wheel.

The gesturing, honking crowd,
a garrulous stream through a forest.

A cacophany of sounds,
bells, yells, horns,
and grating roars;
we listened for signs of
where and when to swerve.

Turning, turning wheel.

Mounds of garbage,
storm drains,
plastic forage for the cows.

Spinning wheel.

The human story of catastrophe
and the means through it.

I hit a man,
apologized.
He shrugged and walked away;

Jaipur was intent,
a prayer wheel spinning.

Wheel.

We couldn't taste the lunch,
or hear the lake breathing;
We didn't savor the Water
Palace of *Man Sagar*
where princes used to fish.

Ashram[1]

Plaid wool under hips,
white shawls and shoulders—
alert repose
where we sat.
We are one,
you are there,
I am that.
Soham.

Still point,
turning world,
breath still,
stirring whirl.

You are that,
I am one,
we are there,
silent in the Himalayan dusk.
Soham.

---

1. The Sanskrit word *Soham* is a mantra pronounced "zo hmmmm" which sounds a little like "so hum." It imitates the natural sounds of the inhalation (zoooooo) and the exhalation (hmmmmm), and it means "I am that" or "I am that I am."

Dhyana

Sit so still you can see the crystals form inside your eyelids;
be with the darkness and enter it awake.

Turn the heat toward waiting without the waiting's end;
be friends with blood and bones to forget they are yours.

Our greatest shrine, this temple, is dressed in cotton rags.
Recall forever (in the meantime): the mountain's whitened crest.

Make peace with death to woo the bright shine of his sister's arms.
Run toward the tunnel but bring its light to rest

upon the forehead
and within,

inside the atman,
behind the skin.

Jams and chutneys

Neem flowers, curry leaves
and a girlboy
make chutney powders.

Girlboygirl is a street child
craving jellies, chutneys and jams.

Orphaned by a stove fire
in a burning flat,
street child craving;

girlboygirl had stirring wizard mother
whirling the hot magenta jam
spooning the coconut chutney
brewing the lemoncurd.

Girlboy streetchild androgyne,
close-shaved hair, baggy clothes
scrawny and solemn,
needs pectin.

Sleeping in the railway station,
girlboy dreams beetroot with tamarind
ridgegourd with crushed peanuts
horsegram with red chili,

streetchild girlboygirl dreams
banana jam with sweet
mother stirring curry on the stove.

Hanuman

1.

We are primates who try to eat the sun
who are punished but saved in the nick of time.
Our luck makes us terrible.

2.

I travel to Sankat Mochan,
shrine to Hanuman, monkey god
of mischief and protruding jaw.

I step in monkey pee
but saunter happily
with a wet left foot
among monkeys and people,
shoelessness and space.

3.

Hanuman thinks the sun is a ripe mango,
takes it in his mouth preventing an eclipse.

Indra throws a thunderbolt,
blasting the jaw of Hanuman
hurls him onto earth.

His father, God of Air, takes away our air, our breath.

Indra relents and
gives Hanuman many boons—
shape-shifting, travel, health, and ease.

He will be immune to fire, weapons, water.

We have no air;
if only water breathed.

Ashoka

"Have I lost or have I won?"
he keened to corpses of the slain.

Ashoka conquered Kalinga,
then thought about his wrongs.

He wrote and taught,
built monasteries and shrines,
inscribed sandstone lion pillars,
sent his children to Ceylon.

Ashoka means painless,
his chakra, a wheel with twenty-four ribs,
on India's flag.

Among thousands and thousands of rulers,
his name alone shines like a star.

What have I done?
he cried aloud to Buddha and the dead.
What have I done?

Meera

When we met I struck the earth with such force,
water gushed out to form a reservoir.

Now you pass the doomed memorials
between the first and second gates,
white marble with semi-precious inlay,
and climb the nine carved storeys of the
Tower of Victory, its dome damaged by lightning.

How can I know so much and yet so little
about you who have called me
to myself and from myself?

I am Meera, I sing my sacred songs,
dance and whirl before the crowd.
Their poison became amrita,
iron nails became petals,
the snake was just a garland.

I am Maota Lake with its saffron gardens:
lawns, stream, and fountain.
Your walls, sandstone of pale yellow and pink,
are amber in the sunshine,
roseate in the moon.

Kalachakra

I have walked your distances,
the universe—

have found no spinning orb
of rock, no more
the sun-bleached retina of ice

a blue-grey circle
a waiting iris, rainbow-lost
an ever-dilated consciousness

packed and shored against
the tide-worn sands.

III

You

> "Thy name
> Among the many sounds alone I heard
> Of what might be articulate."
>
> —P.B. Shelley, *Prometheus Unbound* 2.1.89–91.

Our words are not at all the thoughts we dream

He was someone I knew
but didn't recognize; his face

was lavish as gold
usurping sight,

his hair too thin
to fall across his brow,

thin enough to be
a measure of time.

I fell ten feet on to,
then out of, earth—

there was no sunlight
and there was no reach.

I saw his arms outstretched
from sea to sea;

I touched them,
they became the world;

I touched them, then
I understood a thing.

At your departure

you twirled smiles
into my outstretched arms
again and again.

Felt hat perched and tied,
sphered cheeks bursting with grins,
doll and toast in hand,
packages of worry in the trunk.

Most real body,
pearl, fruit, and feather.

Through the pane of glass,
we make heart-pictures with arms.

I wave salt kisses swallowing hard
blowing circles of air
caught briefly in the wind.

Devolution

We can't afford to love this fiercely anymore.
The west wind off the lake has stopped
hurling noise at our ears. It must
die down, slip to indifferent
summer air

air that doesn't move
but hangs indolent.
Such a love we give,
waiting,

fruit ungathered from branch or ground;
quiet the body,
pretend it's nothing.

Renaissance

Twice you've told me a story of paint:
of a scientist who studies ancient hues,
their composition, their minerals found
in Siena or the vales of Fesole.
It was a documentary you saw
on colors of the Italian Renaissance.

You didn't know you'd told me before—
blue from Florentine flowers, red from Tuscan rock,
your eyes a spinning wheel of lights
for a man who followed colors to their source.

I see vibrant tones of paint on paint,
artist of plant and stucco, harvesting a sun-scorched earth.
I see boxwoods, cypress, lemons, and your smile,
with eyes a harbinger of rebirth.
I think of color, imagine our renaissance,
tracing your lines and contours while you speak

Wrens

My heart is a nest of wrens.
I am old and they are young.

You wrote a searing message
and thought it kind.

This back is a storm-wracked elm,
it is old and I am young.

You cannot see the scars along the bark—
the loggers are not stopped,
on behalf of birds or tree

to marvel at this veined leaf,
my hand, fluttering
heart.

Wanderers roam
through boreal woods.

You think you know what you're doing
not noticing the nest of wrens.

We ask too much of love

We ask too much of love—
when the rain floods
the fields, and the wheat
is past saving

when you cry or
pull away.

We ask that it always work —
an analgesic with no side-effects
an all-you-can-eat buffet
a sun that never sets.

We want it to stay where we can see it
even when it grows small and afraid.

We ask that the dark be imaginary
that all our sighs be understood
and the sky be full of angels.

We ask, or you
ask, or at least I
do

too much of love.

Ramble

I began our
> rural ramble
cautious of your cloud.

For weeks
> you'd brought it home at supper.

cirrus, stratus
> cumulous.

Today we played the game
> positive think/speaking

turning
> the page of
fearful speak/feel.

We scanned
> souwesto sky
for funnel clouds

when we were changed by
> two fawns   leaping

their tails
> white flags
> waving
>> into woodland.

The something then,
> relief   oh
almost—here we go
arrival.

We touched
        hands together

our fingers intertwined
        reading a
new braille.

Your hair was
the color of fawns;
our shirts and their tails
were white flags.

Response

You will think that you are loving
and musing how, you will discover
someone you are not fond of anymore.

When you wake up
from the dream
you will find an unfamiliar body
bits of hair in the sink
crumpled tissues on the floor.

The day arrives duly
as if nothing has happened
when awakened you discover
her scars are your necklace
her tears a pillow of blood beneath your head.

Stellar collapse

I wonder if love is a star
which will collapse some
day, and even then, has infinite density
and curvature of space-time.

All physical theories break
down, at the end
leaving this oneness
our monogamy—
an exclusion principle
prevents our quarks
from becoming
an indistinguishable soup.

And there is no sign
(yet)
of proton or neutron decay;
even in reversed time
odds are
it matters.

IV

Samsara

"Or would they go on aching still
 Through centuries above,
 Enlightened to a larger pain
 By contrast with the love?"

—Emily Dickinson, "Griefs."

Waystation

Giggles bright as droplets
bedew the navy bedspread
and tangle the violet dawn.

Our bedroom is a waystation for wanderers;
unannounced they enter,
round-eyed to see us there,
a cotton kerchief on my hair,
your arm draped on me like a sheet.

The way back is through our room.
We're badly placed for a night of sleep—
resigned to interlopers,
we lie together till morning, when

I make a cardboard model of our life
out of old boxes, yellow and green,
and I write "econo-lodge" in purple paint.

The travellers see the box, but do not smile;
they pause, then hurry on their way.
And so we laugh at ourselves—
at that we excel.

The walls of our house are blank

but in my mind
they are covered with art;

There is a watercolor of a stream
that knows its sounds and shimmers.

There are female and male nudes
(in separate parts of the house);
the male looks strong in pen and ink,
the female, ecstatic in bronze.

There is a photographic collage,
black and white and grey,
snippets of urban scenes spliced
with milkweed seeds aloft.

Pots in swirls of color,
reds, oranges, greens and blues,
next to tiny charcoal drawings of a farm,
chickens smaller than shavings.

Brazilian and Moroccan masks flank
tiles of engraved instruments—
a cello, a sax and a kazoo;

on one wall,
a Persian carpet and a mandolin,
a Miro oil, a waterfall in a glass case.

And in an ephemeral frame
a dream
barely visible
shifting,   never still.

Whoonu?

The game is simple:
you guess each other's favorite things
from these words on yellow cards,

baths or trucks
or corn-on-the-cob?

The game is simple.

Pickles are ahead of long hair if
they're dill and it's not my hair.
They rank after breakfast in bed
if food is served on pottery
with a lone carnation on the tray,
with raspberries, homemade eggs,
freshly squeezed bread
and free-run orange juice.

The game is simple,
if you don't think about it.

Bagpipes outstrip barbequing by a mile
if outside and the day is not hot.
Black is better than most perfume,
but if you comb a cinnamon stick
through your hair for scent
or rub your hands with dried orange peels,
does that count?

The game is not always simple.
Everything has a context.

Snowball fights far exceed cotton candy,
unless the boys from West Flamborough public school
(or people like them)

are in any way involved—
then I'd rather have fake gobs
of pink sticky stuff.

The game is not simple.
It relies on memory.

Between a speedboat and a turtleneck,
I draw a blank, since speedboats can be fun,
but pollute the lake, and breasts squeeze
warmly against the polyester as they itch.
Oysters or crafts? Making crafts better than
eating raw oysters, but smoked oysters
preferable to buying crafts.

you have to choose
you have to choose
you have to choose

"You're not playing right,"
she leaves the room.
The game is simple again.
It's over.

Beginning

In the beginning
a red and white swing
green wading pool
games that splash
tag that freezes
cans to kick
sardines.

In the beginning
well-worn phrases
mud-caked Mary Janes
"girls," "cheese pieces on toast!"

In the beginning
television was black on white
Mr. Dress-up looked like Daddy
but Mr. Dress-up played
all day all day.

In the beginning,
Grandma called us
her little "how-comes":
How come you go to work?
How come you don't play?
How come? How come? How come?

In the beginning
was the number three:
three girls and three blue plastic cups
gingham dresses, paisley drapes, and rabbit plates
beloved but mangled dolls and
their intemperate mothers.

Genesis to exodus
let there be light.
Games that splash, tag that freezes—
let there be light.

Swinging, wading, fading
How come?

Swim the waves

> *I shall roll on and on and on, and break upon your lap with laughter*
> *And no one in the world will know where we both are.*
>   —Tagore "The Crescent Moon"

I run down the driveway to say goodbye
waving at the car's departing guests.

My sister and I follow down the road—
we have been too much alone.

Sometimes she hugs people she barely knows.
They like her though she talks too much,
my mother who has been too much alone.

Together we read books into the night,
peopled with children, animals and love—
freedom in a small space.

I touch a finger to her cheek,
wear her arms in my arms,
feel our pain as one.

We are often alone,
and swim the waves together to the sun.

Doctor Fish

And this is why I read the Amritsar news.

The Gara Rufa, a Turkish fish that feeds on human skin
is the unlikely star of Japanese and Croatian
fish spa resorts—
soles and heels can vacation,
pleasantly nibbled
to cull dead epidermis cells
to revive new skin beneath.

In 2010 the first English fish spa
opened in Sheffield
for patients with psoriasis,
eczema and
other skin ailments

but—and this is important—

according to doctors,
the fish pedicure brings
risk of infection,
blood-borne illnesses,
Hepatitis and HIV.

Though fish and feet,
at the bottom of their worlds
(both ruled by Pisces),
reportedly enjoy
the same salons,
public health decrees:

Think twice before
letting fish feed on your flesh.

Palace El Badi the Incomparable in Marrakech

The pool where the girls were drowned
after Ahmed el-Mansour violated them,
one by one, with his reptilian
body, is empty of water,
void of sunlight.
The pool and palace both empty—

tant mieux
insha'Alla.

As for you who hear me,
you are no Scheherazade, so
please refrain from laughter
at scarred human things,
a hand, a foot, a spine,
a tear-stained face,

life unfinished, pieces
strewn on all sides.

Mammal

Conjoined at birth, love
and murder, incompatible twins.
We tried to separate them
and succeeded
to a point.

Schneiders trucks pound the highway,
snouts barely visible between the bars,
noses and nipples, our shared lineage.

We loved a chicken once;
it sang a joyous chirrup for its seed.
We salivated over it roasted,
in cacciatore, paprikash and fricassee.

Now the hooves we refused to hear are galloping,
thundering now
into pastures and brochures,
polemics and freshly mown hay.

Cows are mudlarks lost along the road,
diffident, unaspiring
nose nuzzles and transient breath.

Southwestern Ontario Gothic

Maybe strong winds colliding
from lakes like oceans—
Erie, Huron and St. Clair—
make such wailing, even in summer when
cornfields and pastures hover in heat

or the earth, impossibly wounded by ice
and snow, tornado too, blinding and alien
in its suddenness

or a peninsular region hemmed in
by water on three sides
possesses an island's danger.

Maybe the Odawa, Ojibwa and Neutral villages
settled for ten thousand years, haunt
their removal.

London is an almost sort of city
spectre of a grander place:
nearly the capital of Upper Canada
but it never was.

Hyde Park, Piccadilly, Westminster, Richmond
a skeleton of names
for an unreported people;

like ghosts, spectral
on the national scene.

Perhaps because settler phantoms
from Scotland, Ireland, the Netherlands
had such faith in hell

the shadow ghosts of peripheral vision
morph from clothed and ordinary
into dense white mist.

V

The Garden Tomb

"In the sweat of thy face shalt thou eat bread, till thou return unto the ground; for out of it wast thou taken."

—Genesis 3:19 KJV.

i cannot tell
for Alice Munro

a woman inside a body
a man behind a woman
solid
seeming

a story behind
the man and woman
a sentence not said
a letter undelivered
meaning missing

a spot of water would show through
quiet as water in a pot

a bridge, a lens, a page
a town, a marsh, a room

surgical
forensic

mirror in mirror
the image sharp and clear
or misted and lost

i cannot tell.

Body Double

Sometimes when I observe
my body in its red swimsuit
tanned in the sun,
the image translates into a prototype,
as if through a camera—
isolated by that propagative lens
of masculine desire.

My eyes have flickered
over my own flesh,
as a stranger's do when
he looks up from his car
in passing the pool where I dive.

His tongue unconsciously wets
his lips and I dive in and suddenly
I am more male than female,
trained by his camera,
a voyeur of the self.

Artemis

1.
Tick ting tangle
a space between
waits;

Proteus gave you a sceptre
to transform and rock space.

2.
I was twelve
when first chained to this rock.
Fleet of foot
you spied me bathing
naked in the woods
and were pursued
torn by hounds.

3.
I am still flying
past the trees
you are still being torn,

as this poem rushes past
both wind and corpse
passion and the rock.

Ash Attic

Her mother's voice across the crematorial sky
into a thin recess where ashes lie,
untrammeled remains.

Time to say the word?
Then say the word.

She looks to find a spark wherever it is
and who is she to blow on it again?
These words are dull as wax, as is her brain,
thick, web-laced attic where she works again,
where worry sits, a broken vintage table,
corroding paint, a thought, that lifts and peals away,
the left leg (like life) too short,
unstable,
it
      wobbles when
its weathered finish is topped with task or wish.

She'd like to write any
any

as she did once
when God spoke clearly
in your cream face and eyes.

She writes one small note to self:
beware of tables, ashes, dust.

Penelope

By a spring beside a pine hut
she sat knitting an unending scarf
and unraveled it each time
she saw the fog descend
or heard the voice of specters in the hills.

She is metaphor or parasite
with the power of philosophy
to open the breaking
world
a figure in mist
illusory and real.

Boat-building

She has to build a boat
to carry family safely through
the summer storm, but she has never
built a boat before.

With charcoal and lead on vellum,
she draws the design,
a likeness of other boats.

Not knowing where to begin, she
goes to the shipyard, talks to builders,
slow-speaking, wrinkled men with watery eyes.
She takes notes, reads blueprints and plans,
collects good pieces of cedar and oak
from broken and abandoned boats, but
the plans confuse her.

At night she dreams
a canopy of leaves and twigs—
a covered wagon taking her across a desert,
for she doesn't know how to build a boat.

So she scavenges an old hull,
weathered and worn with salt,
drags it inch-by-inch,
three nights from shipyard to shore.

She works days at a time without conviction or skill.

She takes her pieces of wood,
hews the roughest seats and oars.
that don't look like seats or oars.

At night she dreams of their old house,
its vast cedar hedge enclosing a sunlit yard;

though passers-by offer advice,
she builds her boat alone.

One day, as if by sudden accident and not design,
the boat is seaworthy, ready for passage,

yet they do not join her—
some have already taken passage on larger ships
out of the harbor in different directions.

She tries to content herself, knowing they are safer than she is
in her handmade boat.

Embarking alone, she
rows under a canopy of leaves,
still dreaming their old home,
a covered-wagon, a cedar hedge,
twigs, and wind-chimes.

Fledglings

Maria leapt to help finches
               flung
by the cat,
orphans scattered on the grass.
She gathered them into a twig-nest,
gaping beaks and pulse of
coal-grey tuft-flecked sides.

She read—
there's no point in rescuing nestlings
(they'll die without their mother).
Fledglings have a chance if
you feed them every hour.

She sent Josephine to dig worms
among the self-seeded onions
of bare April's garden.
She thawed frozen blueberries,
caught flies from kitchen windows.

When Jonathan had a stroke,
she took him places, brought his food,
helped him into bed.

"What's a fledgling?"

"If someone puts it on a finger
and it can hold up its neck,
flutter its wings,
it's a fledgling. If it
can't hold its own head,
a nestling."

She fed them worms,
she marvelled at insatiable
gaping, chirping;

she helped Jonathan to bed,
locked the outside door, turned out
the lights

in darkness
she placed a heating pad on her thin neck.

Tim Beck

Barely half brother
body now broken
doors bolted, then battered,
blood brazenly cold

the police found the body.

Tim
we all tend
toward this catastrophe
(yours)
will finish there.

Last time I saw you
your shirt buttons popped
hair frazzled, slight
stutter, hesitant gait,

you moved us gently
through Hampstead Heath,
Rembrandt, Keats,
roast chicken with garlic and thyme.

You walked like a poem
in manuscript
a draft with markings
egg or splatters of paint
or possibly ink
on the lens of your glasses;

you bore the marks of your revisions
unembarrassed

cooking, artwork, students, words

their coda a surprise
the end-stop unaccepted
by those of us reading
a Tim in progress . . .

I was awaiting the next chapters
the unwritten ones
the hike in the Quantocks
roast chicken contest
trip to Lobo.

The story cuts abruptly
leaves me scrounging for an ending
but there's

no closure
no cadence

no kindness
no Tim.

Ghost

Our neighbor says we have a ghost:
an old woman, gray hair pulled back,
watching at our window.

She says it simply, without alarm—
the ghost is kindly, wears a blue cardigan.

I mistrust the larval words,
yet I struggle to see her furrowed skin,
silvered hairbun and stoic stance
in this empty air, for

there is ever and always some ghost.

She stands on memory's threshold,
waiting and watching for sailing ships,
carts that clatter home,
dark holes in our sleep, and
our turn to be the dead.

VI

Revelation

"And there appeared a great wonder in heaven; a woman
clothed with the sun, and the moon under her feet,
and upon her head a crown of twelve stars."
—Revelation. 12:1 KJV.

Originary

From nothingness
from the
      collapse
     of be-
          fore

left in ruins
defeat, a nexus

longing for

nothing, now

even the sun
        sinks

into numberless stars.

Torn

I practise tearing a particular ligament
in my back, tiny rips, regular, repetitive

treatment of stitch on stitch. This feat
is for you, who pinched my heart

and tossed it into the dense blue;
surprised, the same eye

with which you watched when the muscle in my back
spasmed violently, pushing out our child,

splattered painterly with my blood. Now another heart to lose,
ordeal accomplished. Carrying organs and tearing them is as close

as I allow myself to oblivion. Please do not look so stricken,
so downcast. We all wear our mothers' blood.

new born

one day you'll leave
this imprint,
my shoulder;

we lift you many times

breath-borne we
      raise you to
           light,

eyes
and cream body.

some time, we
yearn for
god-soul,

you are taken,
held rosebud
         aloft.

    carried into
        forward

              toward

        tossed timeward
to glimmerings
honeydew
paradise.

genesis

my mat is more blue
the mirror *mahayana*
the air particulate crystal

upward   facing facing   upward
ceiling lights flicker and vanish

now breath breathes body

kinesis kicking in dolphin dancer's
postures in palmed prayer

maya may murder, but
the sacred mother's mysterious footsteps
pave the world with nothing more lovely
than she is
whose shadow we are

the sunny flesh of the avocado-self ripens
light the oil lamp in your forehead window
and let the ninth child of light birth

the white star on opal blue oceans
stretches into the orbs

a water lily blooms in the shade
urgent vigil
samadhi

forsaken, why oh why?
forever we are born

Core

I was waiting by the apple orchard
and singing for the round nickel of the moon.

The gate swung wide and let me into silence on the ridge.

I don't remember where I went.
Last I saw, I was walking through fountains of corn,
the sky undecided and petaled.

We will dip our hearts again in the red, stained clay.
We will tear rhythm from it like apples.

Sometimes I slept, indifferent to the stains.
Now I know the apples were dances,
the corn a fingerprint, immutable path.

Moksha

We begin with corpse pose.

Is there no kinder word, no lighter note
on which to begin?
It's been a hard week—

push, inhale, stretch
warrior one

inverted v
very very
legs, very arms
        downward-facing
dog, (teeth clench)
relax the face
push into
plank, sweat
on the mat
twenty bodies are one
pouring
their liquid
        salt upon the ground.

Child's pose
sheer forehead
on cool floor.

Such a brow-beating
we normally take
    take
        take

the sutures of mind
        rip
            sutra sutra sutra

only one more breath
then die

a corpse again
thank God
atman
self

Psalm

Although I walk through
the shadow of
the valley of

although we walk through
the death
its shaded, shattered valley
its shadow through

though you are walking
with it, past it
beyond the shadow
of

waters, pasture
you are lying
      down

i am walking
you are still
waters, lying
beside

restoring your
our

lead us not
lead us not into

why the rod and staff?
yet a cup half empty
half full

surely goodness and mercy
surely the valley of the shadow
of the fear will not follow me
all the days of

green pastures
still waters
cup.

Seven-Story Mountain

She climbs the ben,
           the ragged,
jagged brae,
seven stories soaring

to Eden's sunlit peak—

Bounded by southern seas,
the mountain is
the world, its two paths

             up or
                   down

steep bluffs canopy
white spires hover

she scales to surmount

     the top ridge
crested with a stream,
a deep wood,
a griffin's nest,

the discretion of dawn.

Talking to the Unknowable

Tomorrow a gain or loss or truce
will alter the past

and we will reach for signs, particulars,
a keyhole to the future's largesse,

for we bargain that this cleansing action
will leave the crockware of our effort sparkling
inviolate

notwithstanding vandals who could smash
this set of stainless dishes with one blow.

We parry bets and gamble to secure the pact,
brave Faustian bargain with a suffering world,

then rail against the bingo, crap-shoot, lottery of success,
while smeared injustice remains –
yours, theirs, hers
but especially ours.

Causes and effects, knives and white potatoes,
should interact in predictable ways

like the snowflake-laden rocks upon the ground
before the melt,

no wings equal to the aspired flight,
the near-invisible rainbow we barely see—

grant patience in the dancing's frenzied ring
to dancer, dance, and earthen underling.

I took the little book

from the angel's hand
and I consumed it,
I ate the little book.

The angel with the rainbow on his head
laughed and said
you ate the little book.

The seven thunders faded,
the seven candles fell.

The laughing angel turning pink,
then red, white, yellow, then blue,
gave me to understand my belly would be sore
from book-eating, but

the book was sweet like honey.

In the beginning was the word,
flesh
bound.

Face of sun, legs of fire,
the prophecies transpire.

Say the word, now say the word,
sang out my angel crier.

Bibliography

The Dhammapada A Collection of Verses Being One of the Canonical Books of the Buddhists, translated by F. Max Muller, Project Gutenberg e-book: 2008. http://www.gutenberg.org/files/2017/2017-h/2017-h.htm

Dickinson, Emily. *Poems,* edited by Mabel Loomis Todd. Boston: Roberts Brothers, 1896.

Munro, Alice. "The Love of a Good Woman" *The Love of a Good Woman.* Toronto: McClelland and Stuart, 1998.

Shelley, P.B. *Prometheus Unbound.* In *Shelley's Poetry and Prose,* edited by Ronald H. Reiman and Neil Fraistat. New York: W.W. Norton, 2002.

Tagore, Rabindranath. *Collected Poems and Plays.* London: MacMillan, 1936.

Wordsworth, William. *The Prelude: 1799, 1805, 1850,* edited by Jonathan Wordsworth, M.H. Abrams, and Stephen Gill. New York: W.W.Norton,1979.

www.ingramcontent.com/pod-product-compliance
Lightning Source LLC
Chambersburg PA
CBHW051659090426
42736CB00013B/2444